W9-BJE-952

Dear Reader,

Well, it's that time in the millennium where we produce a new issue of everyone's favorite newspaper (drumroll): *The Prehistoric Times!* Most of you won't have even heard of our paper, since the last issue was—well—a few centuries ago...But anyway, rest assured that it's packed with amazing articles, news, and features, as well as a fantastic competition that'll keep you puzzling for years*! Most of it is extremely out of date already, but, hey, when you're a dinosaur with a tiny brain, it takes a long time to put together a whole newspaper. I had to teach myself to write first. And you dinosaurs will probably have to teach yourselves to read. Still, we'll get there in the end. And remember: if you want to know who's who, we've included a handy "Prehistoric Profile" on each page to help you out, and if you get confused about which point in time everyone comes from, just turn to the helpful Prehistoric Roundup at the back.

*Unless you decide to just flip to the Answers pages. But we won't mention that...

Happy Reading!

THE ED

Quarto Knows

Text and illustrations
© Frances Lincoln Ltd 2017
Additional Neave Parker artwork
© The Trustees of the
Natural History Museum, London 2017

First published in the USA in 2017 by
Frances Lincoln Children's Books,
an imprint of Quarto Inc.,
142 W 36th St, 4th Floor,
New York, NY 10018, USA
QuartoKnows.com
Visit our blogs at QuartoKnows.com

Published in association with the
Natural History Museum, London

ISBN 978-1-84780-921-6

Illustrated with mixed media

Designed by Nicola Price • Edited by Eryl Nash
Production by Dawn Cameron
Published by Rachel Williams

Printed in China

9 8 7 6 5 4 3 2 1

CONTENTS

EGG HATCHING SEASON BEGINS

A proud *Protoceratops* mom with her newly hatched brood yesterday. For the full story, turn to page 14.

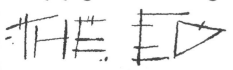

WHERE'S THIS MEGALOSAURUS OFF TO IN SUCH A HURRY?

TURN TO THE SPORTS SECTION ON PAGES 26-29 TO FIND OUT!

DINO? OR DI-NO?

The Committee decides...

King of the beasts, best of the bunch, top of the crop—dinosaurs are the stars of prehistory, and it's no surprise that every critter on Earth wants to be one.

Every year, reptiles, raptors, and even pterosaurs all come along to meet the Dinosaur Committee and find out whether they've got what it takes to hear "Di-yes"—and not "Di-no-sorry-please-come-back-next-year."

Most are disappointed. The things that make a dinosaur a dinosaur have remained unchanged for millennia.

Tyrannosaurus rex, undisputed dinosaur and member of this year's Committee.

have an "elongated deltapectoral crest on the humerus"—whatever that might mean.

"It's not fair," complains one *Hatzegopteryx*, flapping its wings in agitation. "Those dinosaurs think they're so special, but they're not. The differences between us are tiny, really."

"Yeah," agrees a nearby *Ichthyosaurus*, waving a paddle-like fin as it talks. "It's all stuff like what shape their bones are and what angles their bones leave their joints at—that kind of thing. Yawnsville! It's nothing to do with how big and scary we are. I could show that *T. rex* a thing or two. But it's all 'dino-this' and 'dino-that'. That's all anyone seems to

According to the Committee, dinosaurs live on land (not in the sea) and are straight-legged reptiles (meaning their legs stick out beneath them rather than going out to the side, like some lizards), and they also

be interested in."

With so many creatures being left disappointed again this year, we can't help but ask this: instead of trying to be dinosaurs, why don't they celebrate who they really are?

> **"It's all stuff like what shape their bones are and what angles their bones leave their joints at—that kind of thing. Yawnsville!"**

COMPETITION

WIN A YEAR'S WORTH OF FOOD, DELIVERED TO YOUR JAWS DAILY!

Let's face it, whether you like your food green or still dripping with blood, going out to look for it is always a chore.

But just imagine if you could put up your claws, sit back, and have someone bring it to YOU for a change.

Well, that's exactly what we're offering in this issue! All you have to do is complete the puzzles on every page, carve your answers on a piece of rock, and send them in to win a whole year's worth of food brought to you fresh every day! Get puzzlin'!

DO YOU MAKE THE DINO-GRADE?

Why not try our simple, fun quiz to find out?

Are you large, scaly (or even feathery), and quite possibly dangerous? → NO

YES

Do you stand with your legs splaying out to the side rather than directly beneath you? → NO

YES → **Do you live in the sea or a river?** → YES → **Dream on, loser. You'll never be a dino, and that's that.**

NO → **Do you fly?**

YES → **Are you really cool?** → NO

NO → **Duuuude, you're a total dinosaur. Respect!**

YES →

TAIL OF TRIUMPH!

Tamsin, a proud *T. rex*, has recently been announced as the winner of this millennium's Tail-Wrestling Cup.

"I'm so excited to win!" she tells our reporter. "Obviously I beat all the others right away, but that Tess the Titanic put up a strong fight! Erm—can you take the Cup now? My little arms are aching."

Female tyrannosaurs are, of course, larger than the males, who haven't won the Cup—ever.

TYRANNOSAURUS REX PROFILE

LENGTH: 40ft
WEIGHT: 15,000lb

SIZE: They're not the biggest dinosaurs around, but they're definitely one of the scariest (although *Giganotosaurus* and *Spinosaurus* are even bigger and scarier).

PEACEFULNESS: Zilch. These guys are looking for trouble, and they don't care who you are. They're also (whisper it) not very bright. So even if you're a massive sauropod, they might nibble your back leg.

WHAT YOU NOTICE: For such bad boyz (and girlz), *T. rex* have teensy-weensy little arms that can't do much. DO NOT point this out to them or laugh about it. They won't see the joke.

MOST INTERESTING FACT: When they first hatch out of their eggs, baby *T. rex* are covered in feathers—cute! Almost.

LEADERSHIP CHALLENGE

Two *Gravitholus* go head-to-head in battle for top job.

Report by Scrotum Humanum (aka Megalosaurus)

The air is filled with roars, grunts, and earth-rumbling shrieks, as two male *Gravitholus* dinosaurs face each other, ready to charge.

Each is determined to beat the other... and prove himself leader of the pack.

Their names? Nutskull and Thickup Top. Both are a type of pachycephalosaur, with hard, bony, and very thick skulls. These two in particular are well known for being *major* butt-heads.

BUTT-HEADS

"We pachycephalosaurs settle our differences by butting our heads together—hard—until one of us gets a headache and has to sit down," explains a Spoke-o-saurus. "Whether we're fighting over a mate, or over who will lead the pack; it's just the way we do things."

DROUGHT

The *Gravitholus* have been affected by the lack of rain in recent months. "Since the drought, there has been very little food," says the Spoke-o-saurus. "Our leader, Nutskull, thinks rain will come soon, plants will grow again, and we will be able to eat. But Thickup Top thinks the herd should move to find food elsewhere NOW, before it's too late."

While she's speaking, a passing *Troodon* stops. "Wotta buncha boneheads," he sighs, watching the fight. It's well known that troodons are one of the top-ten smartest dinosaurs ever. Although, as the *Troodon* himself chuckles, before going on his way, "Let's face it, mate. That's not saying much!"

② SPOT THE IMPOSTER

We've had recent reports of several dinosaurs daring to pose as our beloved Royal Dinosaur Family's Prince of Prehistorica—and enjoying the perks! To make sure you're talking to the real regal, always check to see that he is carrying all his regalia:

- **CRETACEOUS CROWN**
- **ORNAMENTAL SCEPTER**
- **GOLDEN ORB**
- **MEDAL OF MAJESTY**
- **PRIMORDIAL SWORD**

Find the one-and-only *Regaliceratops* below:

BARRY-ONYX'S FISH BAR

Try our fish sauce— it's a must!

LIKE YOUR FISH FRESHLY CAUGHT AND STILL FLAPPIN'? THEN THIS IS THE *PLAICE* FOR YOU!

OWNER BARRY CATCHES FISH TO ORDER WITH THE HEAVY CLAWS HE'S NAMED AFTER, BEFORE TOSSING IT DAINTILY IN HIS SHARP-TOOTHED JAWS AND STRAIGHT INTO YOUR MOUTH.

BARYONYX PROFILE

LENGTH: 33ft
WEIGHT: 4,400lb

SIZE: Pretty big—about as tall and long as a big tree.

PEACEFULNESS: Depends whether you're a fish or not. Excellent fishermen, *Baryonyx* swing their huge, sharp claws to spear a wriggling fish and then chomp their heads off with their many teeth.

WHAT YOU NOTICE: Their sharp "thumb" claws really stand out—they're quite a bit bigger than the rest of *Baryonyx*'s claws. That's where the name comes from—it means "heavy claw" in Greek.

MOST INTERESTING FACT: Although Barry and his friends are from Europe, they're close cousins with Africa's *Spinosaurus*—they both have long, narrow snouts, just like their aunty Maud.

③ METEORITE SHOWER

It was raining slabs and rocks on the plains earlier today, which caused chaos on the morning commute to the creek. In all, 10 meteorites were observed. Can you spot them all?

④ WANTED

1,000 PEBBLES REWARD!

DEAD OR ALIVE!

Egg hatching season is under way, which means incubation excitement for some...and breakfast for others! One rogue robber has been accused of stealing and chomping on more than 54 eggs. Can you help authorities catch him by drawing the suspect? He was described in the following way:

• BIG BELLY • VERY SMELLY • SUPER-SIZE SKULL • NASTY GNASHERS • TERRIFYING TAIL • LONG TALONS • AWFUL HORNS

ALLOSAURUS OUTTOGETUS!

"Stay alert," warns Dinosaur Committee as predators threaten public safety.

Reports are coming in of an increase in the number of *Allosaurus* stalking and killing other dinosaurs. Several smaller species have been attacked, and one full-grown *Allosaurus* even got the better of a young *Stegosaurus* the other day (see "Fight Report" below for details).

THEROPODS

The killers, part of a group of dinosaurs known as theropods, vary in size, but they all have massive heads, walk on their two hind legs, and have long, strong tails to balance out their heads. They also have weeny little arms that waggle about and look silly, though if you get too close to their sharp claws, you probably won't see the funny side.

TEETH

Allosaurus are known for their sharp teeth, which can grow up to 4 inches long and have a sawlike edge to cut through tough hides. They shed these teeth regularly to make space for new ones. "You can always tell where their hunting areas are because the ground has loads of old teeth scattered around," claims one young *Ankylosaurus* we spoke to. "I was collecting them to make a necklace, but my mom told me they were dirty."

WARNING

Officials say to stay alert and keep an eye out for attackers at all times. Take note of the warnings on these pages, turn the page for some handy tips and tricks...and be safe!

Fighting talk: two Scottish Scleromochlus *reptiles having a dustup in the Late Triassic. Cute!*

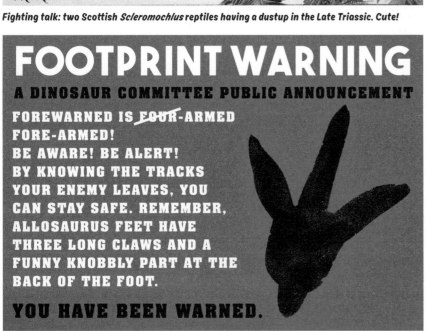

FOOTPRINT WARNING

A DINOSAUR COMMITTEE PUBLIC ANNOUNCEMENT

FOREWARNED IS ~~FOUR~~-ARMED FORE-ARMED! BE AWARE! BE ALERT! BY KNOWING THE TRACKS YOUR ENEMY LEAVES, YOU CAN STAY SAFE. REMEMBER, ALLOSAURUS FEET HAVE THREE LONG CLAWS AND A FUNNY KNOBBLY PART AT THE BACK OF THE FOOT.

YOU HAVE BEEN WARNED.

IN OTHER NEWS... FIGHT REPORT:

Stan Stegosaur vs. Alan Allosaur: Tuesday evening. 3-ton Alan crept up on 2.5-ton Stan and headbutted him hard in his solid side, trying to tip him over. Stan didn't budge and gave Alan a great whack on his back legs with his thagomizer (aka his "knobbly tail"). Alan retaliated with another almighty push, sending Stan onto his back with his hard, pointy spines digging into the dust, his stubby, steggy legs waving in the air and his soft tummy exposed. Stan was stuck and Alan took no time in sinking his enormous fangs into Stan's stomach. Game over. RIP Stanley Stegosaur.

5 ## *ALLOSAURUS* ALERT!

An alert has been issued following an *Allosaurus* sighting—can you escape to the safety of the trees through this maze of teeth and bones?

ALLOSAURUS PROFILE

LENGTH: 28ft
WEIGHT: 3,300lb

SIZE: About as big as a truck (well, when trucks exist one day far from now).

PEACEFULNESS: Low. *Allosaurus* are meat-eating hunters, so let's just say they're not interested in making friends.

WHAT YOU NOTICE: Lots of very long, pointy, sharp, saw-edged teeth crowding out of their mouths. Lots of them. Very, very sharp.

MOST INTERESTING FACT: Like lots of carnivores, *Allosaurus'* teeth fall out all the time. But don't worry, they quickly grow new, even sharper ones. Gulp.

6 # *WHOSE HOOF?*

SPOT THE DANGER BEFORE IT SPOTS YOU!

Learning to identify the footprint of an *Allosaurus* means you'll know when to turn around and run the other way! Can you find the dangerous footprint?

TIPS & TRICKS

It's a rough, tough world out there, and you need to keep your wits about you.

Someone bigger and meaner is always just around the next bush. If you have a keen sense of smell or hearing, get going at the first sign of trouble! Make the most of your camouflage to not get seen in the first place, and lie low. But wits can only get you so far...We visited a local self-defense club for the experts' tips on how to use your natural defenses to stand up to bullies!

See Tony Triceratops in this era's Prehistoric Games–turn to the sports section on p. 26!

BIG IT UP

Scare 'em off before they've started! Making yourself look as threatening as possible will give any attacker second thoughts. Got horns like this *Triceratops*? Point 'em. A neck frill? Stand it up so you look bigger. A fin? Wave it threateningly. Add an impressive roar, and your bullies will soon get going!

COME ON STRONG

If you're already massive, that's a BIG bonus. A huge tail can send opponents flying, and who needs sharp teeth or claws when you can just sit on your enemies? They can't do much squashed under a ginormous behind like this *Cetiosaurus*'s!

PRICKLY CHARACTER

It doesn't matter how hungry you are: nobody wants to pick the bony bits out of their teeth, and a set of spikes like these would make any attacker think twice! Having a prickly back can do wonders for your chances of survival, as this *Scelidosaurus* proves.

FAST ACTION

When all else fails, run awaaay, run awaaaay! Sometimes, the only thing to do is get out of there. Chances are, your attacker is bigger than you and not so light on his feet, so running away, like this little *Ornithosuchus*, may be better than sticking around for the scuffle.

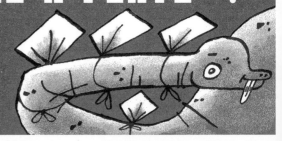

MATCHING

We all have different ways of seeing off the enemy. Can you match each of these dinosaurs to their self-defense feature?

REGALICERATOPS

ARMORED PLATES

DEINOCHEIRUS

BIG NECK FRILL

STEGOSAURUS

SHARP CLAWS

ANKYLOSAURUS PROFILE

LENGTH: 23ft
WEIGHT: 8,800lb

SIZE: About the size of a large van (whatever one of those might be!).

PEACEFULNESS: High. *Ankylosaurus* like eating ferns and moving ve-ery slowly. If they're attacked, they lie down and let their bony armor do the hard work. They're not looking for a fight, but they do have a massive, bony club on the end of their tail that they'll use if anyone gets too frisky…

WHAT YOU NOTICE: The sharp, pointy spikes sticking out from them at every angle. No sharp teeth or claws can penetrate this bony hide, so most ankylosaurs get left alone.

MOST INTERESTING FACT: Adult *Ankylosaurus* weigh 3 to 4 tons and have very short legs, so they are almost impossible to tip over to get a bite out of their soft underbelly—as many a frustrated *T. rex* will tell you.

DOT-TO-DOT

Who is this sharp dresser? Join the dots from 1 to 133 to find out!

⑨ WORD SEARCH

We've turned DD's terrifying prediction into a great activity for all the family! See if you can spot the five catastrophe-related words in the word search below.

METEOR · IMPACT
DUST · STARVE · EXTINCT

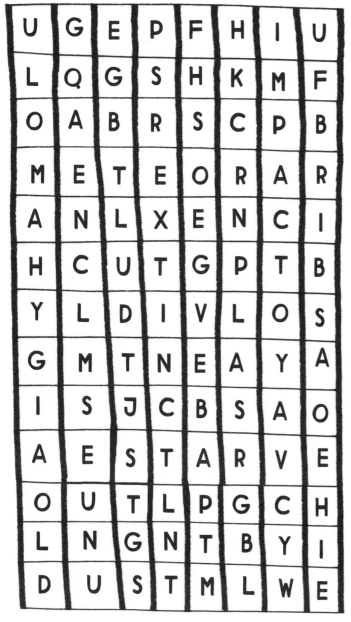

DOOMSDAY DINO PREDICTS DISASTER!

NEAVE PARKER

We've all had our share of catastrophe—whether it's missing your turn at the waterhole, stepping in someone else's dino doo-doo or losing your entire brood of babies to a hungry enemy—it's never fun.

But news is spreading fast about the "Doomsday Dino," a gloomy *Acanthopholis* who claims that a REAL catastrophe is about to strike—and very possibly put an end to everything, including us!

Doomsday Dino—or "DD" as he is affectionately known by his followers—has been telling anyone who'll listen that a giant rock is hurtling toward us from a very, very, very, very, very long way away—and that it's due to hit our ground any century now. We decided to treat his ludicrous story with an open mind and managed to track DD down to find out more...

So. DD, how did you come up with this giant rock fantasy?

It's not a fantasy, I tell you, it's the truth! It came to me in a dream. A giant rock will hit Earth, and send up a dust cloud the like of which has never been seen. The dust and smoke will hang in the air for weeks and months, drowning out all light and warmth from the sun. Nothing will grow, the plants will die, and there will be nothing to eat. First the plant-eaters will starve, and then, when they are gone, the meat-eaters, the hunters, and the scavengers will have nothing to eat and they too will be wiped out forever! Let this word of mine be heard from every corner of the land. We are doomed. Doomed, I say!

Uh-huh. And who exactly is going to throw this rock? Hmm? Giganotosaurus or T. rex might get miffed enough to start slinging stones around, but they're not so big that

⑩ NUR RFO RUOY VLISE!!!

___ ___ ____ _____!!!

DD kindly offered to set one of the puzzles for this page. It's an anagram! Unscramble the letters to find the fun hidden message.

Doomsday Dino claims a giant rock will fall from the sky.

they could throw a rock that big. One of the massive sauropods just might be able to, but they're far too nice and gentle.

No, you don't understand. No one will throw the rock. It will come from up theeeee-re. In the skyyyy.

Oh, like a meteorite? We've seen plenty of those–they're not that big. Sometimes they just bounce off your back! That sorted that out. Enough about giant rocks. What's your favourite color?

[DD doesn't seem to have a favorite color. He looks at us mournfully and shuffles away.]

So, folks–there you have it. Nothing to be scared of; just a silly old dream. The end of our world is NOT nigh, after all, and anyone who thinks one of those little meteorites could make dinosaurs extinct forever, well–they'd have to be as bonkers as old DD. And that's saying something!

ACANTHOPHOLIS PROFILE

LENGTH: 18ft
WEIGHT: 840lb

SIZE: These guys are pretty big herbivores. About the size of something that could be known as a "car" one day in the future.

PEACEFULNESS: High, like most veggies. But there's still the worry that they might accidentally step on you.

WHAT YOU NOTICE: The thick armor and lethal-looking spines all along its shoulders, neck, and spine. If you're after an easy meal, this definitely isn't it.

MOST INTERESTING FACT: Some say they have super-sized guts with special compartments to help digest all the plant matter they eat, producing excessive gas. Wouldn't want to stand downwind from these guys!

FEATURES

SPOTLIGHT ON...
Prehistoric Creatures That Don't Yet Exist But Will Be Really Impressive.

Since dinosaurs make the news so often, we decided it was time to take a look at some of the non-dinosaurs that will inhabit our planet in the future, with the help of our resident psychic, Mystic Megalodon.

JOSEPHOARTIGASIA (GIANT RAT)

First up, imagine what it would be like to come face-to-face with a rodent the size of a bush...Although these will be *vegetarian* rats (phew!), their big buck teeth will be big enough to use to dig in the earth and move large objects, like tree trunks! And that's without even mentioning their heads...which will be over 1.5 feet long. That is one big head for a rat!

MEGATHERIUM

And here we have the Giant Sloth, or *Megatherium*, with its foot-long razor-sharp claws and enormous size. Easily able to knock down a tree to chew on the leaves, this huge creature will also have a fondness for fresh meat. Don't worry too much, though—it'll be pretty slow on its feet, so even if you bump into one in its native South America, you could probably get away with just a light jog.

TITANOBOA

Titanoboa simply means "Giant Snake," and that's exactly what it will be. It'll be so huge, it could eat a one-ton crocodile whole! But it's okay—this jaw-snapping creature will only live in the hot and tropical swamps of South America.

DEINOTHERIUM

Deinotherium have more in common with dinosaurs than you might think—just like "Dinosaur" means "terrible lizard" in Greek, the first part of its name means "terrible," too: "terrible mammal." Armed with a pair of unusually sharp chin tusks, these fearsome-looking creatures will roam around many of the planet's woodlands one day soon, claiming the title of one of the largest non-dinosaurs to walk the Earth. But you can rest easy (unless you're a fern), as they will only eat plants.

PLIOSAURUS
PROFILE

LENGTH: 40ft
WEIGHT: 88,000lb

 SIZE: Huge! About as big as a sperm whale, whatever one of those is…

 PEACEFULNESS: Low. They'll eat anything that comes their way. Their four flat flippers make them speedy, terrifying underwater hunters. BUT, being reptiles and not fish, they have to come up for a breather every so often, so that's your chance to make a getaway.

WHAT YOU NOTICE: These massive marine monsters have extremely sharp teeth, each one about 3 inches long. So watch out next time you go for a swim…

MOST INTERESTING FACT: They belong to the plesiosaur family, but most plesiosaurs have longer necks and smaller heads.

⑪ SPOT THE DIFFERENCE

Study these two pictures of this *Plesiosaurus*, an amazing sea-hunter. There are tiny differences between them: can you spot all **five**?

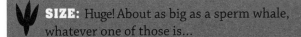

⑫ TEST YOUR GRAY MATTER!

See how many of these questions you can answer correctly.

(True)   OR   (False) ?

1. *Pliosaurus* is a massive fish.

2. *Megatherium* comes from South Africa.

....

3. *Pliosaurus* weighs over 200,000lb.

4. *Titanoboa* lives in woodland.

....

5. *Megatherium* only eats plants.

6. *Deinotherium* means "terrible breath."

....

ARE YOU TINY?
Do YOU want to get bigger?

Then try this simple trick that's making dinosaurs everywhere furious. This is the stuff THEY don't want YOU to know!

It's easy! If there's no bigger creature to prey on and eat you, then you and your family will continue to get bigger…and bigger…and bigger! Simply kill off every carnivorous creature larger than you, and you'll be massive in no time!*

*Small print: This "evolutionary" process will take millions and millions of years.

PROTO-PARENTING

Just look at what this *Protoceratops* mom has to deal with! Not one, not two... but eighteen-y little Protos, all hatching within a couple of days!

"I must admit, it can be tricky knowing where they all are at any one time." Pam smiles, their proud mom. "One wanders off up a dune, another wanders down a dune, and then I hear a crack and know *another*'s on the way." Fortunately, Pam has Paul, her son from a previous hatching, to help out.

FABULOUS FRILL

Paul is almost ready to leave the nest, now he's eight months old. Pam has taught him all her tricks for survival: he's able to find food (mostly

the tough fern stalks that grow in this desert) and he can raise his bony neck frill to make himself look bigger. I ask him to give me a demonstration, and—wow!—Paul will be scaring off the enemies and getting the girlfriends in no time, so ladies, beware!

DANGER

"It's definitely time he moved out," agrees Pam. "I need to concentrate on this lot now. You have to be watching out for danger all the time."

Pam tells us that only last month, 15 little hatchlings were buried in a sandstorm and all of them died. "What a tragedy." Pam nods. "A whole brood at once. Times are tough, but we all expect at least five of our kids to survive."

With that, she looks proudly back at her babies and hurries off to help one struggling out of its egg. Good luck, Pam, and good luck, baby hatchlings!

Pam with Paul, Pierce, Presley, Priscilla, Paige, Pippa, and Prudence.

PROTOCERATOPS
PROFILE

LENGTH: 6ft
WEIGHT: 900lb

SIZE: Teensy, for a dinosaur: grown-up *Protoceratops* are the size of a creature that might exist millions of years from now, called, maybe...a sheep?

PEACEFULNESS: Low. You wouldn't want to get in between a *Protoceratops* and her babies! Even though they don't eat meat, they're known for getting aggressive if they think their offspring are in danger.

WHAT YOU NOTICE: The big, bony neck frill, which *Protoceratops* have to make themselves look bigger and more impressive than they really are.

MOST INTERESTING FACT: *Protoceratops* have massive heads compared with the rest of their bodies, so their mouths are big enough to eat tough stalks and leaves.

Pam is waiting for her last egg to hatch. Draw how you think the little hatchling will look here:

COMMENT:
BY TROODIE TROODON

We've all been there: a push, a crack and it's "goodbye, warm, cozy egg" and "hello, big, bad world." But some baby dinos are lucky enough to have parents who hang around until hatching day to help their little ones get off to the best start, feeding them until they're tough enough to go at it alone.

So why do we have such a bad reputation as parents? Well, because there are always exceptions. *T. rex* are left to fend for themselves from Day One… and we all know what little monsters they turn into. It's the smarty-pants out there who've figured out that looking after their babies

> "So why do we have such a bad reputation as parents?"

means their whole species is more likely to survive. Hippy hadrosaurs live in herds, and sometimes look after each other's babies, while we brainy *Troodon* have even been known to book our babies in for violin lessons.

So I say dinosaurs can make great parents! Let's face it—even tough love is better than no love at all.

WORD SEARCH
Stay close to your nest!

Every year, hundreds of hatchlings are tragically buried in sandstorms or taken by predators. The Hatchling Heroes Association has put together this word search to raise awareness about our little ones. Can you find the **six** words listed?

HATCHING · EGGS · NEST · SAND · INCUBATE · SHELL

H	A	N	H	P	S	E	L	I	Q
A	A	S	F	O	A	T	C	E	R
A	S	T	U	K	N	A	D	G	U
M	A	P	C	B	D	B	F	G	O
T	O	G	S	H	O	U	L	S	F
S	H	E	L	L	I	C	R	B	I
E	I	U	L	A	Z	N	E	U	D
N	E	S	R	O	J	I	G	Y	V

An Apatosaurus yesterday.

HEAD IN THE CLOUDS!

The creatures that roam our planet come in all shapes and sizes, but none are more eNORmous than the peaceful sauropods.

There are many different kinds, but they're pretty much all four-legged plant-munchers with long necks and tails—and they're pretty much all MA-HU-SIVE! Not least the *Argentinosaurus*, which can weigh up to an enormous 70 tons!

We stand on a tree stump and shout up to one of the family, a fully-grown male named Alan, to ask just what it's like to be so…well…huge?

Alan snorts, embarrassed, and a small tree nearby is blown almost to the ground. "I guess," he says softly, "I guess it means that you don't get much trouble. I mean, there aren't many creatures big enough to

> **"We eat a LOT. It takes a large amount of food to fill us up, so most of our day is spent tearing the foliage off bushes and trees."**

bother us, so we pretty much get left alone to do our own thing."

And what might that be, we ask? "Well," he says shyly. "We eat a LOT. It takes a large amount of food to fill us up, so most of our day is spent tearing the foliage off bushes and trees, which we reach with our long necks. But we don't chew. And then we eat some more. And we still don't chew. And then we get a tummyache…My uncle Nagus swallowed some stones once, and we thought he was trying to grind up his food, but turns out it was by accident. The tummyache soon goes away anyway, because we have massive guts for processing our food."

What else does a sauropod get up to on an average day? "Well, we don't move too much— even turning around takes a bit of planning when you're this size, so we just sort of amble forward, eating everything in our path." *Kind of like a sauro*plod? We joke, but Alan doesn't seem to get it. In fact, he appears to have stopped

listening altogether and has swung his enormous neck around to crop another huge mouthful of greens off an unfortunate tree fern. Not a very long attention span, but *sauro*plods or not, these guys are impressive!

A Cetiosaurus from the Upper Triassic on her way for a refreshing dip.

COLOR IN...

...this pretty, feathered *Microraptor* in all its rainbow beauty!

15

ARGENTINOSAURUS
PROFILE

LENGTH: 115ft
WEIGHT: 150,000lb

SIZE: Big enough to shake the ground as they walk!

PEACEFULNESS: Oh, high, high! These gentle creatures live in large herds and look after each other's young! They're not looking for a scrap.

WHAT YOU NOTICE: Their large nostrils, which are important for their good sense of smell and help to cool down their brains.

MOST INTERESTING FACT: They are one of only a few families to live entirely in one historical period: the Cretaceous. No lie!

DUCKBILLS & TRILLS

GOT A HEAD HORN? LIKE TO HONK IT? THEN COME AND JOIN YOUR FELLOW TOOTERS IN THE CRETACEOUS CHOIR.

WE HAVE HONKERS OF ALL SHAPES AND SIZES, FROM HADROSAURS TO PACHYCEPHALOSAURS. SO DON'T BE SHY—COME GIVE IT A TRY!

STEGOSAURUS PROFILE

LENGTH: 30ft
WEIGHT: 6,800lb

SIZE: When fully grown, about 30 feet long. So not that huge compared to some other dinosaurs...

PEACEFULNESS: Pretty high. These herby munchers tend to take it out on trees.

WHAT YOU NOTICE: Erm, hel-lo? That mighty fine double row of plates down the back is pretty eye-catching, wouldn't you say? And the spiky tail is literally eye-catching—as in, "steer clear or you'll lose an eye!"

MOST INTERESTING FACT: *Stegosaurus*'s plates are attached to their thick hides—they're not part of their skeleton like *Spinosaurus*'s plates.

A VERY FINE SPINE!

This issue, we were delighted—and just a little frighted!—to have been granted an interview with the largest flesh-eating dino ever to have walked the earth during our Mesozoic Era— *Spinosaurus*!

Weighing in at a huge 10 tons, this enormous beast is taller than *T. rex*, not least thanks to the stunning sail he sports down his back, which at its highest point measures a good 6 feet high.

We needn't have worried however—Spinky Spinosaur couldn't have been more charming, reminding us in his high, breathy voice that the flesh he likes is mostly fish!

"I swim most of the time, you see," he giggles, wiggling his spine and nearly knocking two low-flying pterodactyls out of the sky. "Fish are my main snack, though I do like some of the smaller plant-eaters, too—depends on what kind of mood I'm in."

Hoping it's a good mood, we begin the interview.

DISHY DINO!

Congratulations to Steve Stegosaur, who came first in this era's Dishy Dino contest.

"We were all taken aback by Steve's plates," gushed one judge. "They demonstrated his maturity and vigor as he strutted the catwalk."

Apparently Steve has had trouble fighting off the ladies for years, blaming his strikingly handsome plates for all the attention he gets.

Steve himself declined to comment on the win, being otherwise occupied with pruning his plates. Nice one, Steve.

And is it true you occasionally have run-ins with *Sarcosuchus*, the giant crocodile?

Yeah, we've had our moments. Mostly we keep out of each other's way, but we both hunt big fish and we've both got a temper, so things have been known to go wrong. Let's just say my great-aunty Sukie didn't die of old age...

We can't help noticing your teeth–you have two long, sharp ones that jut out at the front, and then–would you mind opening for us to have a little look?

Not at all—yes, the ones at the back are pretty sharp, too, but in the middle I mostly have flat ones for grinding up my food. I eat so many different things, you see, I need different teeth to manage. I eat fish, birds, other dinosaurs...pretty much anything that crosses my path.

We decide that now would be a good time to end the interview, and thank Spinky, before making a hasty exit. There's no doubt that they are fascinating creatures, spinosaurs–but probably best viewed from a distance.

So, Spinky–that really is a most impressive sail you have on your back. Can you tell us a bit about it?

Thank you! It's my best feature, really—it has so many uses! Firstly, the girls really like it, so I'm never short of a date. Then it's super-helpful when I'm swimming—I can kind of flick it and it sends me off in another direction—great when I'm chasing fish. But one of my faves is the way I can use it to keep myself cool if it's, like, *really* hot. It's so big that it just lets off all my heat so I can cool down during the day, and because I've stored loads of warmth in it during the day, I can keep myself a bit warmer at night, too.

Wow, that's pretty impressive! You mentioned swimming...tell us more.

Oh, I just love it—I've got all my badges and now I get to dive down really deep and just catch all the big fish down at the bottom of the river. I like being on land, too, but swimming is like...my thing? I have big, webbed back feet so they help me paddle and, like I said, I steer with my sail—and my tail.

> **"I eat fish, birds, other dinosaurs... pretty much anything that crosses my path, really."**

---

⑯ WHAT'S MISSING?

Can you follow these patterns to figure out which parts are missing?

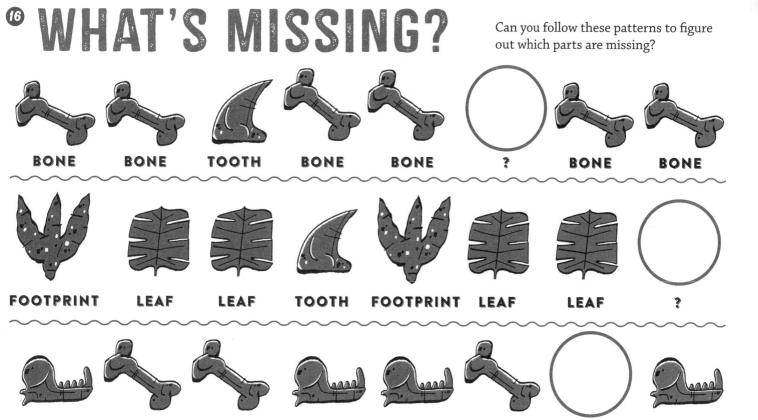

BONE · BONE · TOOTH · BONE · BONE · ? · BONE · BONE

FOOTPRINT · LEAF · LEAF · TOOTH · FOOTPRINT · LEAF · LEAF · ?

JAW · BONE · BONE · JAW · JAW · BONE · ? · JAW

ENVIRONMENT

WILL YOU NEED A RAFT FOR THE RIFT?

We all know that our land, Pangaea—and our sea, Panthalassa—are unpredictable.

One minute you can be standing on a perfectly innocent-looking hill, and the next find yourself tree-high in the air on top of a spurting mud fountain. Or washed away by a dreadful tidal wave. Or buried beneath a landslide. Not to mention sandstorms, earthquakes, avalanches, and sinkholes—it's a wonder any of us dare to get up in the morning.

But did you know this? The very ground we stand on is breaking apart, with huge chunks of it drifting away across the ocean (albeit veeeery slowly).

Maybe we should not be too concerned—this has happened before, after all. According to legend, our land broke apart millions of years ago...and came back together again millions of years later. But this breakup happening now, in our time, will have consequences we may not even have thought of.

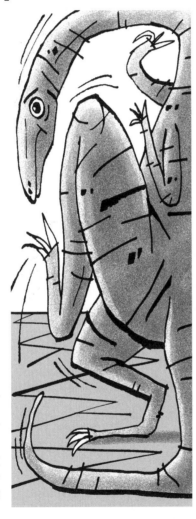

Families may become separated from one another—unless they learn to swim pretty fast. Plants that grow quite happily in the steamy sunshine in this part of the world may die if the land they are growing on floats upward to the chilly north—meaning the herbivores will go hungry and starve. Fewer herbivores will mean less prey for the carnivores, meaning only the strongest, meanest creatures will survive. A scary thought!

So, keep your wits about you, keep your family together, and next time you hear a ginormous rumbling, don't just assume it's your tummy. Watch the ground and do your best to stay on the right side of the cracks!

LYSTROSAURUS PROFILE

LENGTH: 3ft
WEIGHT: 200lb

SIZE: Pretty weeny, depending on how big you are yourself. But let's just say they wouldn't be too tricky to tread on.

PEACEFULNESS: Oh, peaceful! These little guys are herbivores and—let's face it—if you're small enough to tread on, you don't want to go around starting fights.

WHAT YOU NOTICE: They're funny-looking creatures. Only two teeth at the front, like big tusks, and big shoulders on their forelegs, too, to dig their burrows with. Their name means "shovel lizard," which isn't very flattering, but it does the job.

MOST INTERESTING FACT: There are a LOT of these little guys—wherever you go, you can meet one. So when our land breaks up in the way that's been predicted, their family will be broken apart big-time. You have to feel sorry for them...

TRAVEL REPORT:
LESLEY *LYSTROSAURUS* VISITS THE LOWER LAGOONS OF PANGAEA

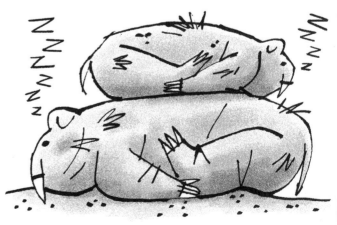

Lazing in the mud, shuffling in the sand, snuffling in the rushes—there are so many ways to relax in the Lower Lagoons that my children and I almost didn't know where

⑰ MAPPING MAD

Can you draw how our land looks during the Triassic period? Copy this picture by using the grids on the square below to help you.

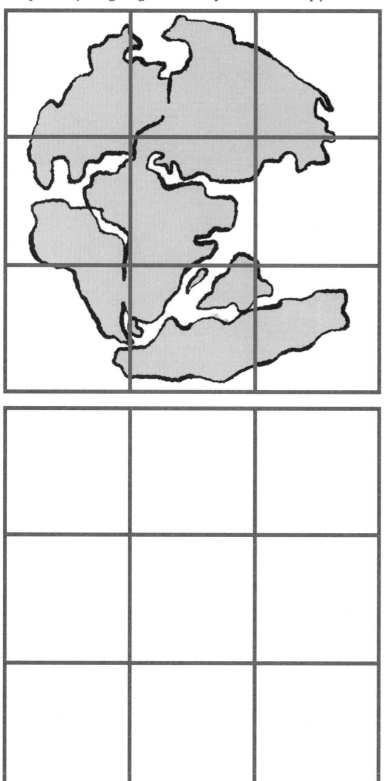

⑱ CRACK-UP CHALLENGE

Here are five pictures of our land as it once was, how it's breaking up, and how it may look in the future. We've numbered the first and last—can you number the rest in the right order?

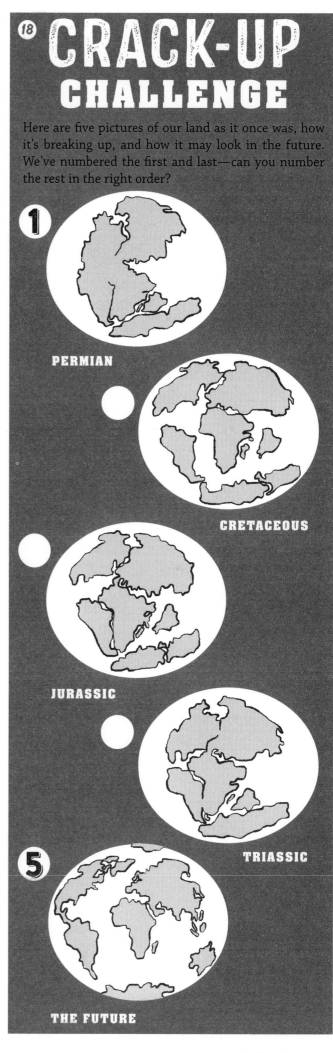

1 PERMIAN

CRETACEOUS

JURASSIC

TRIASSIC

5 THE FUTURE

to begin. After a wonderful day of basking and swimming, it was time to eat—and what a wonderful selection of horsetails and club mosses there was to choose from! After much debate, we opted for a delicious meal of horsetails and club mosses before shoveling three cozy little areas for ourselves in the sand with our powerful shoulders and settling down for a snooze. Our wonderful day by the lagoon was over—but believe me, we'll be back soon!

VERY VEGETARIAN

with Valerie Venenosaurus

This Mesozoic Era of ours has seen many changes, not least to the weather, which—as we all know—affects our plants. We herbivores like nothing more than a huge stretch of greenery as far as the eye can see, but that hasn't always been easy to find. Let's take a look back at some of our main veggie moments.

TRICKY TRIASSIC

During this time—roughly lasting 51 million years (give or take a few hundred thousand)—there wasn't much exciting stuff in the way of greenery. The best ones were around the edges of Pangaea, next to the sea, where there was plenty of rainfall and a bit of saltiness in the air for flavor. The further inland you got, the drier it got until it was practically desert—and the pricklier the trees and bushes became. They'd cut the inside of your mouth if you weren't careful, and you'd be picking spikes out of your teeth for days. NOT the best conditions for a nice salad.

JUICY JURASSIC

Much better! The world really warmed up during this 55-million-year period and became hot and damp—perfect plant conditions. Huge forests grew up all over the place, and trees really started to have their moment, getting big and tall with thick, juicy leaves—mmmm. Ferns, conifers, and ginkgo trees were the main kind, and some of them grew so tall, many vegetarians had to really stre-e-etch their necks to reach—and then stayed that way!

CRUNCHY CRETACEOUS

Yum. This was the longest period—about 80 million years—and during it, the world cooled down again. It got a bit drier, meaning new plants began to spring up—especially ones with delicious flowers such as water lilies and magnolias. Ferns and trees were still going strong, but now there was just more variety, making really excellent salad conditions!

A Diplodocus searches for tasty greens by the edge of a lagoon in the Late Jurassic period.

⑲ PLANT PATTERNS

Look carefully—can you draw what comes next?

GINGKO   **GINGKO**   **FERN**   **GINGKO**   **GINGKO**   **?**

CONIFER   **GINGKO**   **?**   **GINGKO**   **CONIFER**   **GINGKO**

GINGKO   **CONIFER**   **CONIFER**   **GINGKO**   **CONIFER**   **?**

VENENOSAURUS PROFILE

LENGTH: 33ft
WEIGHT: 18,000lb

 SIZE: Medium. With a long neck and tail, they're about 33 feet long.

 PEACEFULNESS: Off the scale! These guys are super-peaceful, lightweight plant-munchers.

WHAT YOU NOTICE: The long neck means they can reach up to the high branches of trees and bushes. A long tail helps them balance so they don't tip over.

MOST INTERESTING FACT: The name means "poison lizard" but there's nothing poisonous about these guys—they're named after the area of North America that they come from.

⑳ VEGGIE HUNT

Test your veggie-hunting skills and see if you can find all **six** hidden words!

**GINKGO · FERN · CONIFER
SALAD · SPIKY · JUICY**

L	A	D	A	T	C	B	U
G	I	N	K	G	O	F	J
S	O	H	S	O	N	H	U
A	E	B	F	L	I	B	I
L	G	D	E	R	F	A	C
A	V	L	R	S	E	O	Y
D	E	U	N	Z	R	C	O
L	S	P	I	K	Y	S	T

HOMES & PROPERTY

PEEK INSIDE...

After the success of last issue's focus on Fanny Ferganasaur's fabulous fern-filled home in the woodlands of Central Asia, we were delighted to be invited to view the cave of Pterry and Ptanya Pterosaur in this issue.

Perched high on a rocky outcrop, Pterry and Ptanya's comfy cavern boasts views of both the ocean and the lush landscape behind. "It's so wonderful seeing the sun go down over the horizon." Ptanya smiles. "Watching Pterry diving for fish against an orange sky is just magnificent."

AWKWARD

So, we asked, just what is it that pterodactyls look for in a home? "Can I just stop you there?" says Pterry apologetically. "Everyone calls us 'pterodactyls' and leaves off the 'us'? But we're actually *Pterodactylus*. It's a small point, but important to...well...*us*. And while we're on the subject, don't even think about calling us 'dinosaurs.' We're actually a type of flying reptile—NOT dinosaurs—so let's get that out of the way before we go any further." We duly apologized, and awkward moment over, Pterry moved on to answer our question.

FISH SUPPERS

"So, we generally live by the coast," he explained. "We're big fans of fish, see. As fliers, we can also reach these high-

up areas on the cliffs that you couldn't get to by foot, so we don't have to worry about predators."

Taking us deeper into the cave, Ptanya proudly points out her charming collection of fish bones and, of course, the nest, where two little ones squawk eagerly for food. Fondly, she vomits up her meal into their mouths.

KIDS

"Pteresa here is two." She points to her eldest, who begins preening her feathers proudly. "She learned to fly quite recently. And Ptom is my baby—it'll be another couple of years before he's ready to fly the nest."

With a final admiring glance around the craggy, dank corners of the family's cave, we make our way out into the sunshine and say our farewells. It's hard to imagine a more cozy and welcoming home than a *Pterodactylus*'s, and we look forward to another visit sometime soon!

㉑ TEST YOUR KNOWLEDGE!

Read these pages, then decide whether these statements are true or false:

1. *Ferganasaurus* **live in the desert.**

2. *Pterodactylus* **are herbivores.**

3. *Pterodactylus* **mostly live in caves by the sea.**

4. *Hatzegopteryx* **from the Late Cretaceous period are teeny tiny.**

THE TREE TREND

There's no denying it! The Cretaceous period is seeing a sharp rise in the number of trees growing across the planet...

And with them comes new shelter, new diets, and new habitats for those of us small enough to find a home in their branches.

Of course trees have been around for a long time, but the gradual change in climate to a more wet and tropical atmosphere has given them the ideal conditions for growing, and seen them enjoy a huge comeback in lots of different varieties. So just what is so great about trees?

"Well," answers a young *Microraptor*, who has developed just the right curved claws and feet for climbing sheer trunks, "trees make great lookouts, give protection from predators and amazing views—not to mention being comfortable places for a snooze in the sun!"

And with that endorsement, it looks like trees are becoming hot property. Check them out in your neighbourhood today!

A young Hypsilophodon trying out a tree yesterday.

---

22 LITTLE PTERESA HAS GONE FOR SOME FLYING PRACTICE, AND NOW SHE CAN'T FIND HER WAY HOME AGAIN! CAN YOU HELP HER GET BACK TO HER WORRIED MOM?

PTEROSAURS
PROFILE

LENGTH: around 36ft
WEIGHT: 550lb

SIZE: This can vary massively between the different types of pterosaurs—from *Pterodactylus*, who's usually the size of a big bird, to the enormous *Quetzalcoatlus* or *Hatzegopteryx* of the late Cretaceous period, who grew as big as a small "plane" (some sort of flying machine that doesn't exist yet).

PEACEFULNESS: Medium. Pterosaurs eat mostly fish and small creatures, so if you stay out of the water, you've got a better chance.

WHAT YOU NOTICE: The large, bony crest on the back of their heads. Do they use it to steer with in the wind? Or just to impress everybody? Whichever it is, we're impressed!

MOST INTERESTING FACT: They walk on four legs on land, not their two back legs. And, though many of them are covered with feathers, they will not—we repeat, NOT—develop into birds.

IT'S GAME TIME!

*Report by
Andy
Ankylosaur*

One of the most popular events in the prehistoric calendar, the Prehistoric Games bring together the biggest and the best.

Drawing crowds from all over Pangaea, it's a chance to marvel at the sheer, brute strength of some of our biggest dinosaurs and non-dinosaurs, to wonder at their wit (or lack of it), and to try the really good saliva sauce at Barry Onyx's traveling Fish Bar. And Barry definitely did not give me a free burger for saying that.

In this report, Andy Ankylosaur takes a look at this year's top contenders, and talks to winners...and losers...in the most exciting event of the millennium.

SUPER STRENGTH

Ian *Iguanodon* gives a proud thumbs-up to his mom after it is announced he's the winner in the Vegetation-Thrashing Contest. (Though, truth be told, his thumbs always look like that). In Ian's contest, competing herbivores were required to flatten an area of bushes and small trees in the shortest time—Ian completed it in under a minute. Well done, Ian!

23 DOT-TO-DOT

Join the dots from 1 to 78 to reveal the winner of the Hoopla event, reported on the pages 28-29 (don't cheat by turning the page!)

SENSATIONAL SWIMMING

Congratulations to Iggy *Ichthyosaurus*, a marine reptile who bagged the top slot in the non-dinosaur swimming races, competing against other top-notch non-dinosaur floaters such as the toothy *Ischyodus* and the even toothier *Enchodus* (known by his friends as "the saber-toothed herring" because of his big fangs). Looking at Iggy's sleek, streamlined body, tail, and flippers, you could be forgiven for thinking the *Ichthyosaurus* is a prehistoric fish. He LOOKS very like a fish, but the truth is, *Ichthyosaurus* have lungs and need to pop out of the water every so often to breathe. "That's true," gasped Iggy when we caught up with him, "but on this occasion I kept jumping out because those guys kept nipping my tail. I've never swum so fast in my life trying to get away from them!" Well, whatever the reason, Iggy, it won you the top prize—congratulations!

DODGY *DIPLODOCUS?*

Once again this year, complaints abound about allowing some of the larger sauropods such as Denny *Diplodocus*, to compete in the 100-meter race. "It's ridiculous!" snarls a little *Velociraptor* called Valerie. "We're fast, but we don't stand a chance against a brute that size. We're only about 3 feet long, and they're about 175 feet! All they need to do is shuffle forward a few steps and they've won!" Experts argue that some sauropods' brains are so small, they don't always realize they're even in the race, giving other contestants a fair chance. But the Athletics Committee has agreed to discuss this issue once again.

24

MATCH THE MEDALS

See if you can match up each of these five pairs of medals, exact replicas of those from the Prehistoric Games!

TURN THE PAGE FOR MORE GAME RESULTS!

HOOPLA HEROES!

The air is hushed and atmosphere tense as Tony *Triceratops* takes to the field for one of the most anticipated events of the games: the Hoopla.

A sport that tests not only agility and accuracy but also endurance, as contestants sometimes compete for days on end in an attempt to beat Jurassic athlete Polly *Polacanthus*'s record score of 14 hoops at once.

"To be fair," comments one onlooker, "Polly had an advantage since she had at least 14 spikes for hoops to land on. And Tony here only has three. And anyway, I heard that..." Our commentator is stopped as a bystander shushes him; the action is about to begin. On the field, a bellow signals the start of the event, and Tony lowers his head to catch the first throw of hoops. It's likely that the onlooker was about to remark on the widely discussed theory that Polly wasn't even a contestant in the Jurassic Games, but simply in line for a snack.

We'll never know for sure, but the usually peaceful herbivore Tony *Triceratops* will be butting trees tonight in frustration—he missed beating Polly's record by just one hoop. Good try, Tony—better luck next time.

Polly Polacanthus, legendary winner of the Hoopla during the Jurassic Era.

Tony Triceratops lowers his horns in preparation for the first throw of hoops. His final score was 13.

㉕ COLORING COMPETITION

Color in this drawing of the rainbow-feathered *Velociraptor* in all her glory.

IN OTHER SPORTS NEWS

Commiserations to Mark *Megalosaurus*, who was disqualified from the 400-meter race by running fast—in the wrong direction...

Mark is reported to be feeling "distraught" at the referees' decision.

²⁶ FLASH QUIZ

TEST YOUR KNOWLEDGE OF THIS MILLENNIUM'S GAMES WITH THIS QUICK QUIZ:

1. True or false? *Ichthyosaurus* is a large fish.

....

2. How many hoops did Polly *Polacanthus* catch on her spikes during the Prehistoric Games?

....

3. True or false? Tony *Triceratops* is carnivorous.

....

4. How long is a full-sized sauropod? A) 80 feet B) 250 feet C) 175 feet

....

IGUANODON PROFILE

LENGTH: 33ft
WEIGHT: 17,000lb

SIZE: Not enormous, but he's a very respectable 33 feet long and weighs about 8 tons. You wouldn't want him to roll on you.

PEACEFULNESS: High. As herby munchers, *Iguanodon* try to tackle tall trees, not *T. rex*.

WHAT YOU NOTICE: The spiky thumb, of course! What's it for? No one's sure! Poking predators in the eye? Ripping through tough leaves? It's anyone's guess.

MOST INTERESTING FACT: *Iguanodon* spends most of its time on all fours, but it can rear up and run on its back legs. OK—call it "*really* interesting fact."

COMPETITION ANSWERS

How did you do in the puzzles? Have you sent your answers carved in a rock to enter the competition? If you have, check them against the right answers here. And if you haven't, ummm… please don't copy these ones?

2

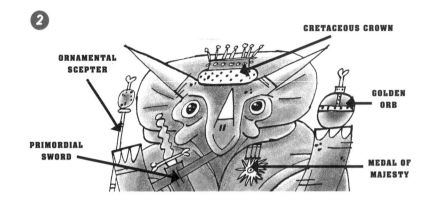

CRETACEOUS CROWN

ORNAMENTAL SCEPTER

GOLDEN ORB

PRIMORDIAL SWORD

MEDAL OF MAJESTY

3

5

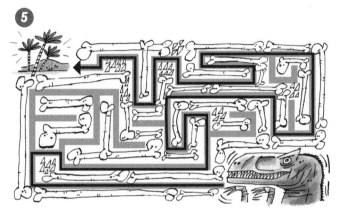

6

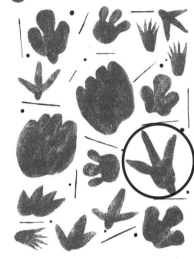

7

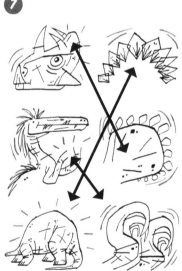

8

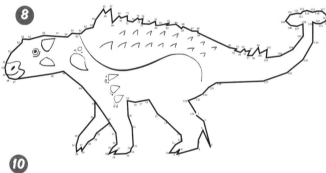

9

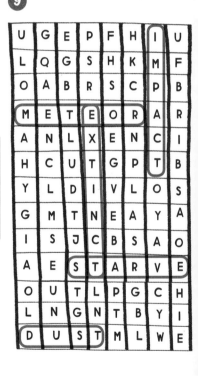

10

NUR RFO RUOY VLISE!!!

RUN FOR YOUR LIVES !!!

11

12

TEST YOUR GRAY MATTER!

True OR False ?

1. *Pliosaurus* is a massive fish.

FALSE—REPTILE

2. *Megatherium* comes from South Africa.

FALSE—SOUTH AMERICA

3. *Pliosaurus* weighs over 200,000lb.

FALSE—88,000LB

4. *Titanoboa* lives in woodland.

FALSE—TROPICAL SWAMPS

5. *Megatherium* only eats plants.

TRUE!

6. *Deinotherium* means "terrible breath."

FALSE—IT MEANS "TERRIBLE MAMMAL"

14

16

BONE	BONE	TOOTH	BONE	BONE	TOOTH	BONE	BONE
FOOTPRINT	LEAF	LEAF	TOOTH	FOOTPRINT	LEAF	LEAF	TOOTH
JAW	BONE	BONE	JAW	JAW	BONE	BONE	JAW

19

GINGKO	GINGKO	FERN	GINGKO	GINGKO	FERN
CONIFER	GINGKO	CONIFER	GINGKO	CONIFER	GINGKO
GINGKO	CONIFER	CONIFER	GINGKO	CONIFER	CONIFER

18

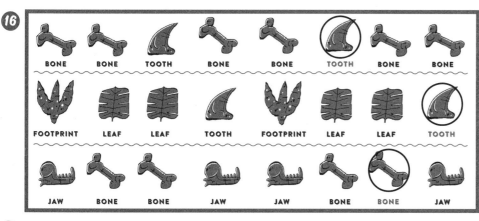

CRACK-UP CHALLENGE

Here are five pictures of our land as it once was, how it's breaking up, and how it may look in the future. We've numbered the first and last—can you number the rest in the right order?

1 PERMIAN

4 CRETACEOUS

3 JURASSIC

2 TRIASSIC

5 THE FUTURE

20

L	A	D	A	T	C	B	U
G	I	N	K	G	O	F	J
S	O	H	S	O	N	H	U
A	E	B	F	L	I	B	I
L	G	D	E	R	F	A	C
A	V	L	R	S	E	O	Y
D	E	U	N	Z	R	C	O
L	S	P	I	K	Y	S	T

21

TEST YOUR KNOWLEDGE!

Read this page, then decide whether these statements are true or false:

1. *Ferganasaurus* live in the desert.

FALSE—THEY LIVE IN THE WOODLANDS OF CENTRAL ASIA

2. *Pterodactylus* are herbivores.

FALSE—THEY EAT FISH

3. *Pterodactylus* mostly live in caves by the sea.

TRUE!

4. *Hatzegopteryx* from the Late Cretaceous period is teeny tiny.

FALSE—IT CAN GROW AS BIG AS A SMALL PLANE

23

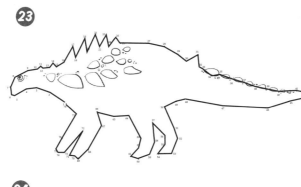

22

24

26

FLASH QUIZ

TEST YOUR KNOWLEDGE OF THIS MILLENNIUM'S GAMES WITH THIS QUICK QUIZ:

1. True or false? *Ichthyosaurus* is a large fish.

FALSE—IT IS A MARINE REPTILE

2. How many hoops did Polly *Polacanthus* catch on her spikes during the Prehistoric Games?

14

3. True or false? Tony *Triceratops* is carnivorous.

FALSE—HE IS HERBIVOROUS

4. How long is a full-sized sauropod?
A) 80 feet B) 250 feet C) 175 feet

C

PREHISTORIC ROUNDUP

Confused about the Cretaceous? Boggled by *Baryonyx*? Let's face it, getting your head around who lived when can be pretty challenging...so we've made this useful little guide to help! Just keep in mind that "MYA" means "million of years ago."

THE DINOSAURS:

ACANTHOPHOLIS *"Spiny scales"*
Lived: 115–91 MYA (Early Cretaceous)

ALLOSAURUS *"Other lizard"*
Lived: 156–144 MYA (Late Jurassic)

ANKYLOSAURUS *"Stiff lizard"*
Lived: 74–67 MYA (Late Cretaceous)

ARGENTINOSAURUS *"Argentina lizard"*
Lived: around 90 MYA (Late Cretaceous)

BARYONYX *"Heavy claw"*
Lived: around 125 MYA (Early Cretaceous)

CETIOSAURUS *"Whale lizard"*
Lived: 170–160 MYA (Middle Jurassic)

DEINOCHEIRUS *"Terrible hand"*
Lived: 120–110 MYA (Early Cretaceous)

DIPLODOCUS *"Double beam"*
Lived: 155–145 MYA (Late Jurassic)

FERGANASAURUS *"Fergana valley lizard"*
Lived: 166–157 MYA (Middle Jurassic)

HADROSAURUS *"Big lizard"*
Lived: 78–74 MYA (Late Cretaceous)

HYPSILOPHODON *"High-ridge tooth"*
Lived: around 125 MYA
(Early Cretaceous)

IGUANODON *"Iguana tooth"*
Lived: 140–110 MYA (Early Cretaceous)

LYSTROSAURUS *"Shovel lizard"*
Lived: 250 MYA (Early Triassic)

MICRORAPTOR *"Tiny plunderer"*
Lived: 125–122 MYA (Early Cretaceous)

ORNITHOSUCHUS *"Bird crocodile"*
Lived: around 185 MYA (Late Triassic)

OVIRAPTOR *"Egg thief"*
Lived: 88–70 MYA (Late Cretaceous)

PACHYCEPHALOSAURUS *"Thick-headed lizard"*
Lived: 76–65 MYA (Late Cretaceous)

POLACANTHUS *"Many spines"*
Lived: around 125 MYA
(Early Cretaceous)

PROTOCERATOPS *"First horned face"*
Lived: 85–80 MYA (Late Cretaceous)

REGALICERATOPS *"Royal horned face"*
Lived: around 68 MYA (Late Cretaceous)

SCELIDOSAURUS *"Limb lizard"*
Lived: 208–194 MYA
(Late Triassic to Early Jurassic)

SPINOSAURUS *"Thorn lizard"*
Lived: 95–70 MYA (Late Cretaceous)

STEGOSAURUS *"Roof lizard"*
Lived: 156–144 MYA
(Late Jurassic to Early Cretaceous)

TRICERATOPS *"Three-horned face"*
Lived: 67–65 MYA (Late Cretaceous)

TYRANNOSAURUS REX *"Tyrant lizard"*
Lived: 67–65 MYA (Late Cretaceous)

VELOCIRAPTOR *"Swift robber"*
Lived: 75–71 MYA (Late Cretaceous)

VENENOSAURUS *"Poison lizard"*
Lived: 125–112 MYA (Early Cretaceous)

THE NON-DINOSAURS:

DEINOTHERIUM *"Terrible beast"*
Lived: 11–1 MYA
(Miocene to Pleistocene)

ENCHODUS *"Spear tooth"*
Lived: 90–50 MYA (Late Cretaceous to Early Eocene)

ICHTHYOSAURUS *"Fish lizard"*
Lived: 250–95 MYA
(Early Triassic to Late Cretaceous)

ISCHYODUS *"Strong hold"*
Lived: 168–3.6 MYA
(Middle Jurassic to Late Pliocene)

JOSEPHOARTIGASIA *"Fossil rat"*
Lived: 4–2 MYA (Pliocene)

MEGATHERIUM *"Giant beast"*
Lived: 35 MYA–11,000 years ago
(Eocene to Holocene)

PLESIOSAURUS *"Almost lizard"*
Lived: 245–65 MYA
(Middle Triassic to Late Cretaceous)

PLIOSAURUS *"More Lizard"*
Lived: 251–65 MYA
(Early Triassic to Late Cretaceous)

PTEROSAURS *"Winged lizard"*
INCLUDING *QUETZALCOATLUS*, *HATZEGOPTERYX*, AND *PTERODACTYLUS*
Lived: 228–66 MYA
(Late Triassic to Late Cretaceous)

SARCOSUCHUS *"Flesh crocodile"*
Lived: around 112 MYA (Early Cretaceous)

SCLEROMOCHLUS *"Hard fulcrum"*
Lived: around 217 MYA (Late Triassic)

TITANOBOA *"Titan boa"*
Lived: 60–58 MYA (Paleocene)

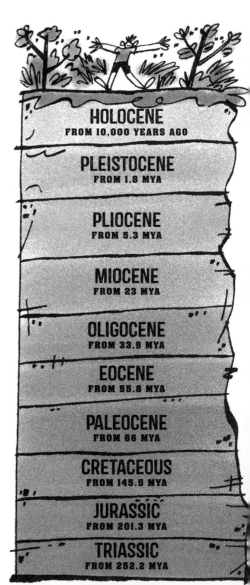

HOLOCENE FROM 10,000 YEARS AGO

PLEISTOCENE FROM 1.8 MYA

PLIOCENE FROM 5.3 MYA

MIOCENE FROM 23 MYA

OLIGOCENE FROM 33.9 MYA

EOCENE FROM 55.8 MYA

PALEOCENE FROM 66 MYA

CRETACEOUS FROM 145.5 MYA

JURASSIC FROM 201.3 MYA

TRIASSIC FROM 252.2 MYA